EMOTIONS
by
Caleb Merritt

Cover designed
by
Maurice Ingram

Published by Mocy Publishing, LLC
Copyright © 2012 by Caleb Merritt. All rights reserved. Except as permitted under the United States Copyright Act of 1976, no part of this publication may be reproduced or distributed in any form or by any means, or stored in a data base or retrieval system, without the prior written permission of the publisher. This book is also available in print at most of your book retail stores.

**Discover other titles
by
Caleb Merritt
at Mocybox.com**

- Dedication 4
- My Book Acknowledgements 5
- NIGGA 6
- Get On My Level 7
- Tell me 8
- Prelude 10
- Being Fake 11
- What I Want From You 12
- A Secret to Tell 13
- The Light 14
- I Wish 15
- The Song 16
- Why Are You Afraid 17
- Why? 18
- LIFE 19
- Jesus Christ 20
- Consecrate Me 22

Dedication

This book of poetry is for every human being regardless of age, that has every felt unloved, unappreciated, or like an outcast that does not belong. I want to let you all know. You are Loved. You are appreciated, and you do belong. And in Jesus Christ you will always have a special place in his heart. I hope these poems bring you inspiration to never give up.

Your Loving Friend,
Caleb J. Merritt

My Book Acknowledgements

I would like to thank my Lord and Savior Jesus Christ, for giving me the strength and patience to persevere every day of my life, and for giving me the gift of writing. All praises, honor, and glory flow to you. I love you always. Your servant Caleb.

To my parents, Shedrick and Carlean Merritt. Thank you for raising me on the word of God, and thank you for all you do for me.

To My High School Journalism & English Teacher, Ms. Kathryn Joyner. Thank you for putting me on the path of writing poetry. I'll never forget it.

To Mocybox, thank you for seeing beauty in my writing, and for publishing it.

And inspirational thanks to my favorite writers, Margaret Walker (For your beautiful novel Jubilee) Langston Hughes (For your Phenomenal poem Genius Child) To Edger Allen Poe (For your extraordinary poem The Raven)
and Geoffrey Chaucer (For your sensational novel The Canterbury Tales) May you all rest in peace.

And a very special thanks to all my fans and readers. I Love you all.

NIGGA

Nigga…Yo Nigga…Nigga!

Man, why the fuck you not answering me? I said Nigga!

(Sigh)…Oh my bad…human being…

Answer- Yes, how may I help you?

Get On My Level

You couldn't understand my sexual notions,

Even if I lubed them up with lotions,

And I busted in the warmth of your inner brain,

And made the intelligence on my sperm cells rain.

Now that we've established that I'm too much for you,

Your ignorance is now and forevermore through.

Don't be mad cause you can't understand a man like me,

And there's a limit in life to what a nigga like you can be.

Many try, few succeed. The only thing you'll ever be good at, is selling a bag of weed.

Tell me

Tell me, tell me how to be.

When life's storm clouds rain over me.

Tell me, tell me what do you do?

When so called friends just up and betray you.

Tell me, tell me how to receive, positive energy while I grieve.

Tell me, tell me why shouldn't I cry,

 When living life, can make you want to die.

Oh Lord my God, my strength, my savior.

Please deliver me from these foolish thoughts and behavior.

Tell me, tell me how to live. Teach me, teach me how to forgive.

Tell me, tell me what to say,

When I get on my knees to consult you and pray.

There are many things I don't understand,

So, I beseech you to lend me a helping hand.

So tell me, tell me how to love,

So that I may join you up above.

Prelude

This is a prelude of my happiness and sorrow.

So listen up, as I may not be here tomorrow.

This is a prelude I sing with joy.

The joy of an innocent and helpless little boy.

This is a prelude I give with my heart.

Which so many people have tried to tear apart.

This is my prelude filled with love, as pure as the white on a heavenly dove.

This is my prelude as gentle as a flower, but also as broad as a sea or a tower.

This is my prelude that resounds so loud.

The angels sit and listen on the edge of the clouds.

This is my prelude that will pierce and protrude.

This is my prelude, kind and not rude.

Being Fake

You laugh with me, and smile in my face,

But when I'm not around that's not the case.

You say a lot of vulgar things about me.

Saying I really think he's gay, don't you agree?

So the bottom line is, if that's how you feel.

Don't smile in my face BITCH BE REAL!

What I Want From You

First you look into my eyes, showing me where my future lies.

Then you lusciously lick your lips, while caressing my body with your fingertips.

Suddenly you grab me with a dominate force, making dick extremely hard of course.

By now your authority has been proven true, and you can make me do anything you want me to.

The touch of your hands chills my soul, and the thickness of your manhood makes my body explode.

As you penetrate me we both grow excited, and you grab me once again saying baby don't fight it.

I think to myself, what if this is all just a dream? Damn I hope not because that's how it seems.

But as we both climax reality hits, and you lean over and say damn that was some good shit.

A Secret to Tell

There is a secret I need to tell,

But I don't know if you'll receive it well.

I have many things I want to say,

And I'm losing time day by day.

A lot of people wouldn't think it, because of how masculine I am,

But really on the inside I'm as soft as a lamb.

I need to tell you because I've found someone.

A person I found to be a lot of fun.

A person I would love to wake up to everyday,

So all there is left to say is I'm gay.

The Light

I need to find the light, to get out of this dark place.

Hoping to one day feel, a loving warm embrace.

I need to find the light to see what's around,

Because evil has viciously knocked me to the ground.

I need to find the light to come out of sin,

And glorify God so the devil won't win.

I need to find the light.

Regain knowledge and sight.

I need to find the light.

The light that shines so bright.

I Wish

I wish I could tell you that I love you.

I wish I could tell you I want you to be my boo.

I wish I could tell you how deep my emotions run,

Because when I see you my heart smiles brighter than the sun.

I wish I could hold you tight in my arms,

And keep you by my side as a good luck charm.

I wish I could tell you of all the sleepless nights.

I stayed up thinking if my love for you is right.

I wish I could tell you I adore and cherish you.

I wish I could tell you I think your sexy too.

I wish I could hit you with cupid's arrow and not miss,

But most of all I wish I could give you a big kiss.

The Song

The song is long.

The song is strong.

The song is to be song, among.

People who frown, people who cry,

People who can't quite understand why.

The song is long.

The song is strong.

The song is to let you know what's wrong.

Why Are You Afraid

Why are you afraid of my sexuality?

Is it because you wish you were me?

Why are you afraid of my personality?

Is it because you wish you could be with me?

Why are you afraid of how I talk?

What concerns you about my walk?

Do you want me to whisper I love you in your ear?

What is it about me you really fear?

Why are you so critical of how I act?

Is it because you like me, which is a fact?

You made me feel inferior.

You made me feel small.

You made me feel you didn't want me at all.

But when it comes down to it, you really do.

So baby I think the confused one is you.

Why?

Why sit in the midst of shadows, or in the darkness of space?

Not knowing where I am, the time or the place.

Why kneel and bow to the trials of being alone?

With a faintly cry and a docile tone.

But…why expect to heard when there is no light,

And every ounce of hope is completely out of sight?

Why have a mind of wisdom and a heart of love?

When it seems you've been forsaken by the almighty above…

So…why do this and why do that,

When the outcome of life is never exact.

LIFE

A mind numbing pain, a mind numbing sorrow,

Who cares for love or what's to come tomorrow.

If life is beauty and beauty is life.

Why is everyday lived with overbearing strife?

The end.

Jesus Christ

Where is it the truth lies?

Maybe in our souls and maybe in our eyes

Or could it be in an innocent child's cries.

Where does our faith lie?

Is it in our hearts deep down when we pray?

Or living life unafraid day after day?

Where exactly does your love lie?

Is it in a sexual image imbedded in your mind?

Or knowing someone has truly treated you kind.

Where is it your strength is found?

Maybe from pain that has torn you down?

Or knowing one day you'll receive a heavenly crown.

Ask me how truth, faith, love, and strength coincide.

They're all things that are needed worldwide.

And in knowing where they come from, we want to be precise,

And the answer is simple, our Lord and Savior Jesus Christ.

Consecrate Me

Consecrate my heart; let it pour out to thee.

Calling on your name commands the devil to flee.

Consecrate my mind; let it be stable and pure.

Not doubtful, not wild, insane or unsure.

Consecrate my strength; help me to persevere

And not kneel and cower in the comfort of fear.

Consecrate my feet; teach me to walk with pride.

Having humility in each step, and love in every stride.

Consecrate me Lord. Consecrate me every day.

Consecrate me please, as I walk my Christian way.

About Caleb

Biography

Born on the eastside of Detroit Michigan, March 29, 1989. Caleb Merritt wrote his first poem in the eleventh grade. He was inspired by his high school Journalism teacher, and ever since then in the world of writing, the sky has been the limit. He has written four screenplays and is in the process of writing three novels. Coming from a very musical background as well.

Caleb is also a serious Jazz Vocalist and sings, Classical Jazz music. "Emotions" is his first of many volumes of poetry to come.

www.ingramcontent.com/pod-product-compliance
Lightning Source LLC
Chambersburg PA
CBHW071458070426
42452CB00040B/1887